Heredity

By Myrl Shireman
Illustrated By John E. Kaufmann

ISBN 1-58037-373-9

Printing No. D04132

Mark Twain Media, Inc., Publishers
Distributed by Carson-Dellosa Publishing Company, Inc.

Level 6: Book 3

Heredity

Imagine two mother cats with new kittens are enjoying the sun. Their kittens are playing close by. One mother cat is yellow, but her five kittens are many different colors. The other mother cat is black. All of her five kittens are black. Why is one group of cats all black? Why are the other cats many different colors? One must study **heredity** to find the answers. Heredity explains why family members often look alike. It also explains how physical characteristics are passed from parents to children in families.

Genes

To understand heredity, one must learn about **genes**. There are thousands of cells in our body. Genes are found in the body cells. Each of us has 46 **chromosomes** in every cell of our body. Chromosomes are long strings of DNA found in cells. DNA is like a messenger. It tells the chromosomes the traits that each of us will inherit. Human genes are arranged as 23 pairs on the chromosomes. Each pair has a gene from the father and a gene from the mother. Therefore, each of us gets one-half of our genes from each parent. It is genes that give us hair color, eye color, and height. The things that we inherit, like hair color, eye color, and height, are called **traits**. Each of us may inherit traits that are not as visible as hair color, eye color, and height. Traits like color blindness and certain diseases may also be inherited.

Mendel's Pea Plants

Long ago, people wondered why animals and plants often looked alike over many generations. A monk named Gregor Mendel wanted to find out why. He began experimenting with short and tall pea plants. He chose pollen from a group of pea plants that had been short for many generations. He then took pollen from different pea plants that had been tall for many generations. He placed the pollen from the short plants into the flowers of the tall plants. Then he placed the pollen from the tall plants into the flowers of the short plants. This is known as **cross-pollination**.

Gregor Mendel cross-pollinated tall and short pea plants.

Mendel found that the first generation of cross-pollinated plants were all tall. He then planted seeds from these plants. These seeds were the second generation of cross-pollinated pea plants. When these seeds produced pea plants, not all of them were tall. Three out of four of the plants were tall, but one out of four was short. Mendel knew there must be a reason why most plants were tall but others were short. Mendel had discovered how genes work. It was the plants' genes that made some plants tall and some short.

Dominant and Recessive Traits

Each gene has two **alleles**. The alleles determine the traits that will be inherited. In Mendel's original peas, each gene had two alleles. In the tall peas, the two alleles in the genes for height were both for tallness (*TT*). In the short peas, each gene for height had two alleles. The alleles in these peas were for shortness (*tt*). When the tall and short pea plants were crossed, the plants that grew from these seeds each had a gene for height. The gene had one allele for tallness and one allele for shortness (*Tt*).

First-generation plants

The alleles make a gene dominant or recessive. The **dominant**, or stronger, allele's trait overrides other traits. A **recessive**, or weaker, trait will only appear if both alleles are recessive. Capital letters are used to represent dominant traits (*T*). Small letters are used to represent recessive traits (*t*). If both alleles in the genes are *TT*, then the plant will be tall. If one allele is *T* and one allele is *t*, then the plant will also be tall. Tallness is the dominant trait. The plant must have two alleles for shortness (*tt*) for the plant to be short.

The tall pea plants from which Mendel took pollen had genes with both alleles dominant for tallness (*TT*). The short pea plants from which he took pollen had genes with both alleles recessive for shortness (*tt*). However, the cross-pollinated plants of the first generation had genes with one dominant allele for tallness (*T*). Each plant gene also had one allele recessive for shortness (*t*). The gene alleles for each plant were *Tt*. The plants that grew from these *Tt* seeds were all tall. The gene's allele for tallness (*T*) was dominant.

To get the second generation, Mendel crossed two of these tall plants that had a tall and a short allele (*Tt*). When the seeds from these plants grew, three out of the four plants were tall. One plant was *TT*, and two plants were *Tt*. One out of the four plants was short. It had two alleles for shortness (*tt*).

Traits in People

Look around at your friends. Look at all of the traits they have inherited. Do you notice that some have brown hair? Some have hair of another color. There are some people with blue eyes. Some have brown eyes. You have tall friends and short friends. Why do we have different eye colors? Why are some people tall and some are short? What about hair color? Each of us gets one-half of our genes from our father. The other half of our genes comes from our mother. Each gene has two alleles. One allele is from each parent. The alleles in the genes carry the traits that will show up in the child.

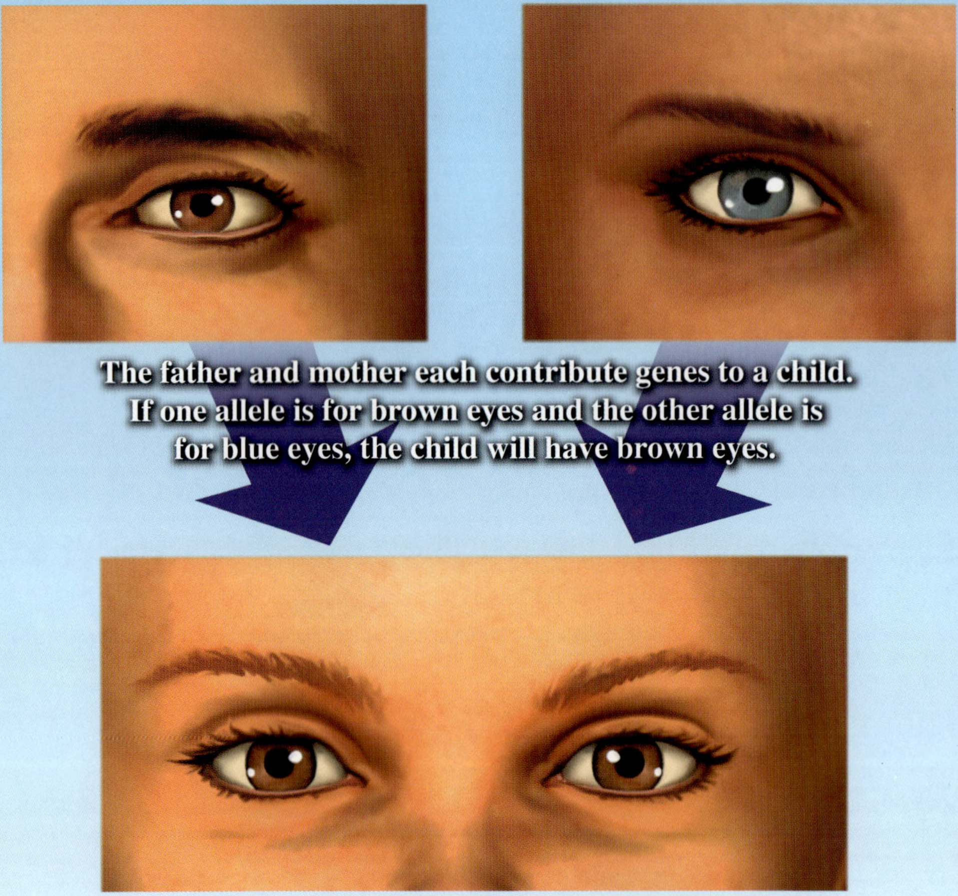

The father and mother each contribute genes to a child. If one allele is for brown eyes and the other allele is for blue eyes, the child will have brown eyes.

When both alleles in the gene for eye color are for blue eyes, the child will have blue eyes. What happens when the pair of alleles for eye color are not the same? The allele in the gene from one parent may be for blue eyes. The allele in the gene from the other parent may be for brown eyes. The eye color of the child will depend on the gene's dominant allele. The allele for brown is dominant over blue. The child will have brown eyes. The recessive allele for blue eyes is present in the gene, but the eyes will not be blue. What if the alleles in a gene are both recessive for blue eyes? Then the child will have blue eyes.

Find a mirror and look at your ear lobes. Do they hang freely? You will find that some people have ear lobes that hang. Others have ear lobes that are more attached to the side of the head. The gene for hanging ear lobes is dominant. If you have ear lobes that do not hang, you have inherited two recessive alleles. Do you have dimples? If you do, you have inherited a dominant allele. If you do not have dimples, you have inherited two recessive alleles. Hair color is determined the same way. Remember, for a recessive trait to appear, both alleles on a gene must be recessive.

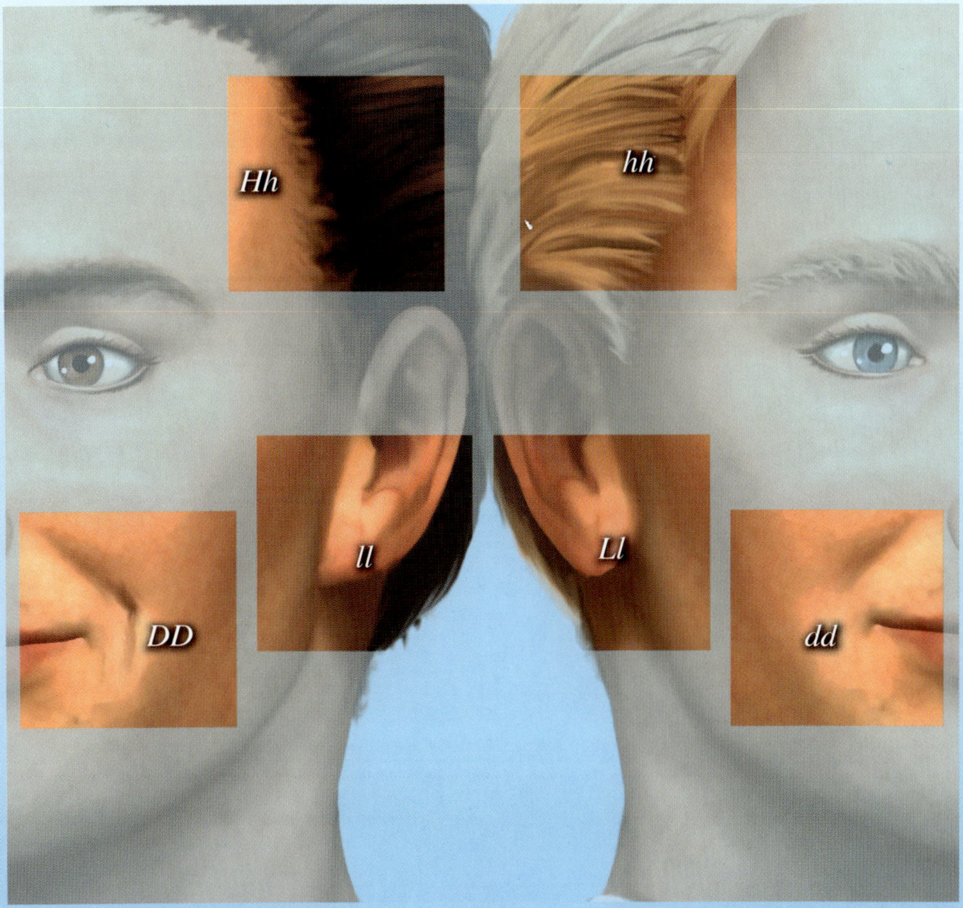

Codominant Traits

Sometimes, a gene may not have a dominant allele. The two alleles may be **codominant**, or equally strong. Pink tulips have codominant alleles. One of the alleles is for a red tulip (*R*). The other allele is for a white tulip (*W*). The gene would be *WR*. The two traits are blended. The resulting **offspring**, or next generation, is a pink tulip.

Recessive Alleles

How can you tell when there is a recessive allele present? A recessive trait only shows up when the alleles from the mother and the father are both recessive. What if a mother and father cat both carried one dominant allele for a long tail and one recessive allele for a short tail (*Ls*)? If four baby kittens are born, three might have long tails like the mother and father. If one of the kittens has a short tail, you would know that both parents were carrying the recessive allele for a short tail. The alleles in the genes for the short-tailed kitten would be recessive (*ss*).

Phenotype and Genotype

There is a name for the way an animal or plant looks. The name is **phenotype**. A brown kitten has a phenotype of brown. The kitten's color is brown. A white kitten's phenotype is white. The phenotype for a certain tree might be rough bark, while another tree may have smooth bark.

There is another special name to know. The name is **genotype**. The genotype means the actual traits contained in the genes. You cannot always tell the genotype by looking at a plant or animal. A brown kitten has a phenotype of brown. However, the kitten may carry a recessive gene for another color. So the genotype might be *Bw*.

Variation and Mutation

Recessive genes cause **variations**, or differences. Blue eyes, blond hair, and no dimples are all variations. They happen very often. Sometimes, there is a change that is not a variation. There is a change in the DNA in a gene. When this happens, the DNA sends the wrong message. This causes a **mutation** in the gene. This is a sudden change in inherited traits.

Once, all watermelons had seeds. Then a watermelon grew without seeds. This was a mutation. Now watermelons without seeds are common. Mutations can create new, helpful traits. However, some mutations can be harmful to the plant or animal. Scientists study genes to try to understand how these changes occur. They hope to be able to prevent harmful mutations.

Heredity explains how family members sometimes can be easily recognized. We share certain traits and physical characteristics. Yet, each person has his or her own unique look.